# My First Book about the Animal Alphabet of Europe

# Amazing Animal Books
# Children's Picture Books

## By Molly Davidson

## Mendon Cottage Books

*JD-Biz Publishing*

Read More Amazing Animal Books

Purchase at Amazon.com

# Download Free Books!
# http://MendonCottageBooks.com

#  is for an Appenzeller Dog.

The Appenzeller was bred as a herding dog, first in Switzerland.

Today, they are used for farming as well as a rescue dogs in many Swiss mountains.

 **is for a Boxer.**

Boxers are a head strong bred, originally bred in Germany.

They were one of the first dog breeds to be used in police work in Germany.

# **C** is for a Chamois.

The chamois is a mountain goat that lives in the European mountains of Austria, Italy, Switzerland, Turkey, and Romania.

The boys mostly live alone, but the girls and babies live in herds, to help protect each other.

# D is for a Dachshund.

Dachshund are stubborn dogs, they do not train very easily, and were first bred in Germany.

They are very loyal and loving towards their owners; they have a loud bark so they also make wonderful guard dogs.

 **is for an Edible Frog.**

Edible frogs live in calm rivers and streams in central Europe.

These frogs only eat meat; like insects, other frogs, spiders, moths, flies, fish, newts, and sometimes birds.

In France, frog legs are served as a national dish.

**F is for a Ferret.**

The ferret was first had as a pet 2,500 years ago in Europe; it was used to hunt rabbits.

Ferrets sleep for a total of 18 hours per day, and they sleep in 6 hour shifts.

Wild ferrets eat mice, rabbits, and small birds.

# G is for a Glow Worm.

Glow worms live in woodlands and caves.

Only the girls can glow, they will glow about 2 hours each night trying to attract a boy.

 **is for a Hedgehog.**

The hedgehog has been around for over 15 million years; it lives in Europe, Africa, Asia, and New Zealand.

They only weigh about 4 pounds, and run, at top speed, around 12 mph (19 km/h).

# I is for an Irish Setter.

The Irish setter, nicknamed Big Red, was bred as a hunting dog in Ireland.

They are in the top ten for best dogs to have as pets, because of their active, outgoing, and sweet natured personalities.

 **is for a Jack Russel Terrier.**

They were first bred to hunt foxes in Germany.

Jack Russel Terriers were bred for working, thus they are very energetic, active, intelligent, athletic, and fearless.

 **is for a Kingfisher.**

Kingfishers live around freshwater rivers and lakes.

They can lay up to 10 eggs at a time and both the mother and father incubate the eggs for about 3 - 4 weeks before they hatch.

# L is for a Long Eared Owl.

The long-eared owl lives in the forests of the northern hemisphere.

They live between 40 - 60 years in the wild.

 **is for a Maltese.**

The Maltese was bred 28 centuries ago in Malta.

The Greeks have thousands of paintings and art of the Maltese; they even made tombs for them to be buried in.

 **is for a Norwegian Forest Cat.**

The Norwegian Forest cat lives in the north of Europe, in the cold, Scandinavian region.

They have long fur, weigh about 22 pounds, and are gentle and loving.

 **is for an Olm (Cave Salamander).**

Arne Hodalic© Wikimedia Commons

They live in underwater rivers that flow through limestone caves, in southern Europe.

Olm's are blind, live all their lives in the darkness of caves, and eat insects, worms, larvae, and snails.

# P is for a Purple Emperor Butterfly.

The purple emperor lives throughout most of Europe in the woodlands.

Only the boys have purple/blue wings; and unlike most butterflies, they eat oak sap, not flowers.

 **is for a Queen Elizabeth Pocket Beagle.**

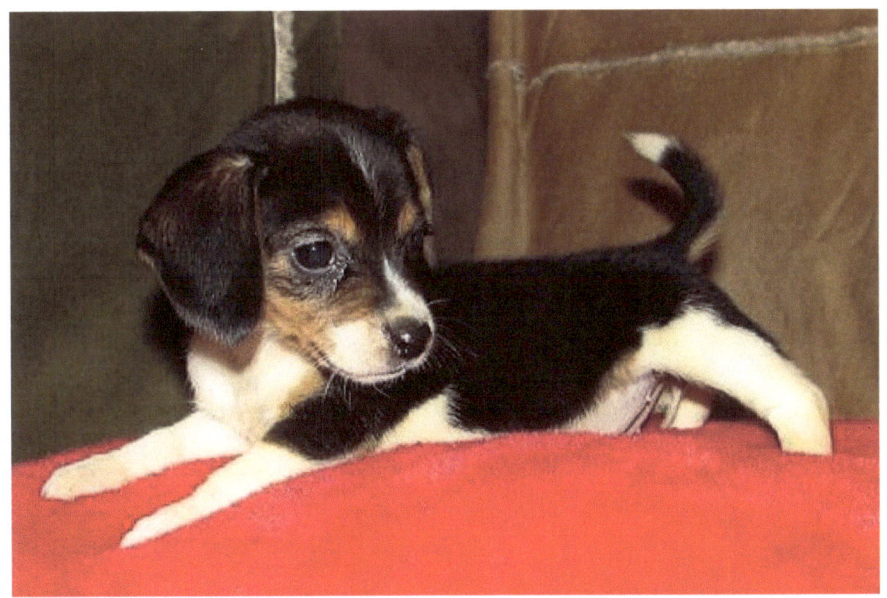

The Queen Elizabeth pocket beagle is a newer bred of hound, now bred as a lovable pet.

Pocket beagles were originally bred, in medieval times, to fit in a saddle pocket to be used to help chase animals from their dens, so they could be hunted.

#  is for a Reindeer.

Reindeer, also called caribou, live around the Arctic Circle and the North Pole, in Asia, Europe, and North America.

They will use their hooves, to dig through the snow and ice, in the winter, to find food.

# S is for a Flying Squirrel.

Flying squirrels live in forests all over the World.

Interestingly they cannot actually fly, they just spread their arms and legs and leap from tree branch to tree branch.

# T is for a Turkish Angora.

The Turkish Angora cat was first bred in Turkey.

They have blue eyes, and some have one blue eye and one yellow; and thick white fur.

# U

is for Ursus Arctos, the scientific name for a brown bear.

Brown bears live in the northern woodlands and mountains of Europe, Asia, and North America.

They are one of the largest bears in the world; they can weigh up to 860 pounds!

# V

**is for a Vulture.**

The vulture is a scavenger bird found all over the World, except Australia and Antarctica.

They have very excellent eyesight; they can see a carcass from 4 miles away in a cloudless sky.

#  is for a Wild Boar.

Wild boars live in the forests of Europe, Asia, and Africa.

They usually sleep about 12 hours, during the day, and then they eat at night.

They are able to run up to 30 mph (48 km/h).

 **is the last letter in the animal red foX.**

The red fox is one of the most abundant foxes found in the north around the Arctic Circle, in Asia, Europe, and North America.

Their tails are almost as long as their whole body, about 2/3 the length.

# Y  is for a Yorkshire Terrier.

Yorkshire terriers are a small dog, weighing about 7 pounds, and are bred in Great Britain.

**Z** is for **Spalax Zemni, the scientific name for a Podolsk Mole -Rat.**

**Bassem18 © <u>Wikimedia Commons</u>**

The Podolsk Mole-Rat lives in Central and Western Ukraine.

In 2008, they were put on the IUCN Red List of threatened species.

---

**Horses** For Kids
Amazing Animal Books For Young Readers
By John and Annalee Davidson

**Ponies** For Kids
Amazing Animal Books
Rachel Smith

**Ten Amazing Horses** For Kids
Nature Books for Kids
JD-Biz Publishing
K. Bennett

**Akhal-Teke** "The Golden Horse of the desert" For Kids
Nature Books for Kids
JD-Biz Publishing
K. Bennett

**Suffolk-Punch** "The Gentle Giant" For Kids
Nature Books for Kids
JD-Biz Publishing
K. Bennett

**Shires** "The great Horse" For Kids
Nature Books for Kids
JD-Biz Publishing
K. Bennett

**Colonial Spanish** "Horse of the Americas" For Kids
Nature Books for Kids
JD-Biz Publishing
K. Bennett

**Canadian** "The Little Iron Horse" For Kids
Nature Books for Kids
JD-Biz Publishing
K. Bennett

**Cleveland Bays** "History and Future" Horses For Kids
Nature Books for Kids
JD-Biz Publishing
K. Bennett

**Our books are available at**

1. Amazon.com

2. Barnes and Noble

3. Itunes

4. Kobo

5. Smashwords

6. Google Play Books

## Download Free Books!
## http://MendonCottageBooks.com

# Publisher

JD-Biz Corp

P O Box 374

Mendon, Utah 84325

http://www.jd-biz.com/

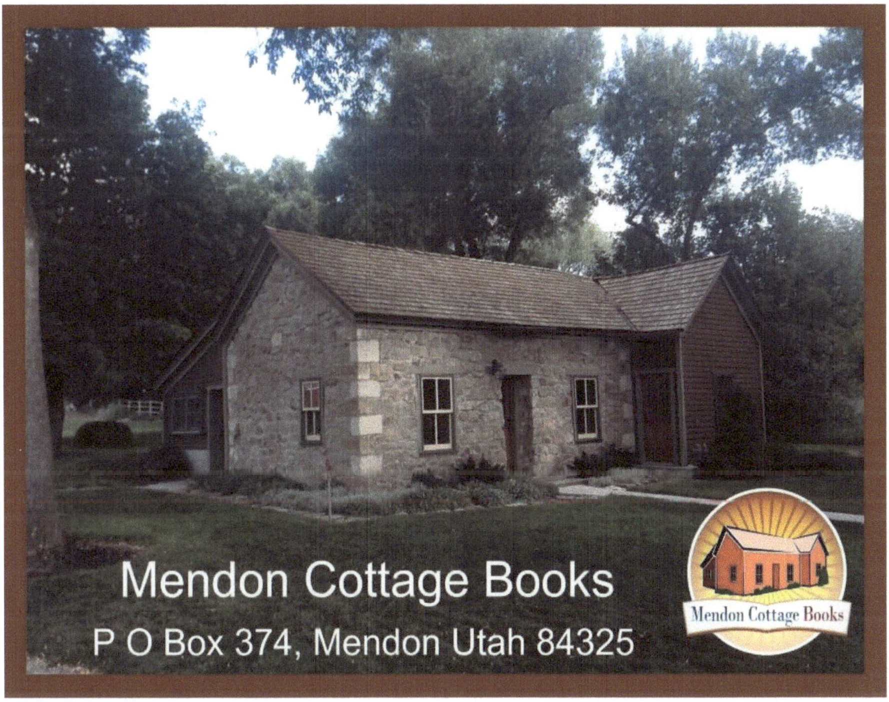

Mendon Cottage Books

P O Box 374, Mendon Utah 84325